FERTILITY TECHNOLOGY

The
Baby
Debate

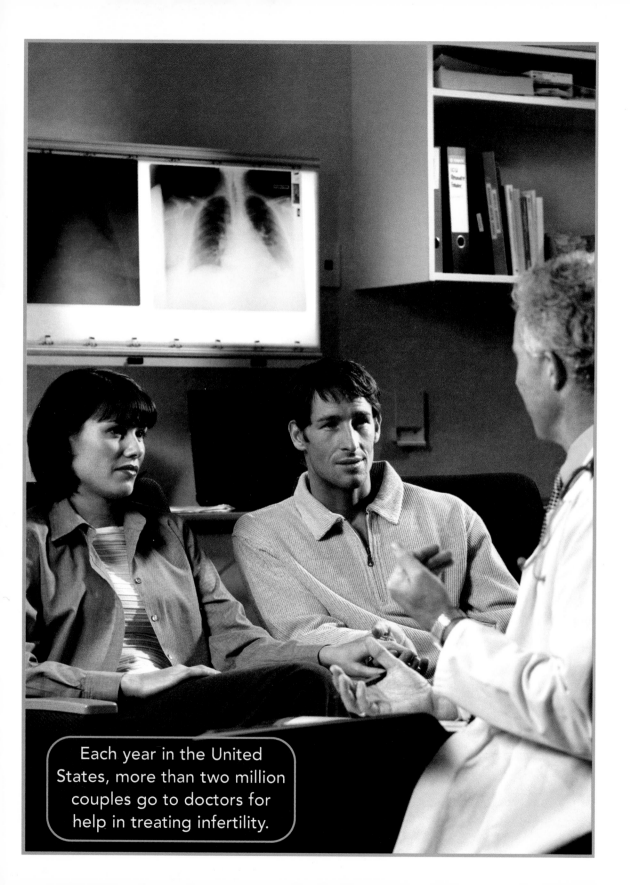

Each year in the United States, more than two million couples go to doctors for help in treating infertility.

FERTILITY TECHNOLOGY

The Baby Debate

Kara Williams

The Rosen Publishing Group, Inc.
New York

For Quent.

Published in 2000 by The Rosen Publishing Group, Inc.
29 East 21st Street, New York, NY 10010

First Edition

Cataloging-in-Publication Data

Williams, Kara.
    Fertility technology : the baby debate /Kara Williams.
      p. cm. —(Focus on science and society)
    Includes bibliographical references and index.
    Summary: Describes the important ethical, legal, and scientific questions that arise about fertility technology as medical science continues to progress.
    ISBN 0-8239-3210-9
    1. Fertility technology—Juvenile literature. 2. Medical science—Ethical and legal aspects—Juvenile literature. [1. Fertility technology. 2. Medical science.] I. Title. II. Series.

2000
660.6—dc21

Manufactured in the United States of America

CONTENTS

Louise Brown, the first child conceived with in vitro fertilization, was born in 1978.

INTRODUCTION

Mark, a lawyer, and Simone, a high school principal, were married when they were both in their mid-twenties. They knew they wanted to be parents someday, but they chose to put off having children so that they could focus on their careers. They wanted to be financially stable—out of debt and in their own house—before they brought children into the world. When they reached their early thirties, they realized that many of their friends were already raising kids and thought, "It's time."

For a year, Mark and Simone tried to conceive a child without any luck. Simone said to herself, "There's something wrong with me. Why can't I have babies?" Mark figured that with their hectic work schedules, perhaps they were both too stressed out to conceive a baby on their own. They decided to consult a doctor who specialized in helping couples have children.

FERTILITY TECHNOLOGY: THE BABY DEBATE

After several tests, the doctor determined that Mark and Simone had some medical problems that prevented them from conceiving naturally. First the doctor prescribed certain drugs for Simone so she would ovulate regularly. When the drugs did not help Mark and Simone conceive, the couple tried a medical procedure called intrauterine insemination (also known as artificial insemination). After several failed attempts, the doctor suggested a more technologically advanced medical procedure—in vitro fertilization.

This time, the treatment was successful, and four years after Mark and Simone first started trying to have children, they were able to hold their darling twin girls in their arms. Though the years of medical treatments were often disappointing, not to mention stressful to their marriage and their bank account, Simone says the end result

Timeline

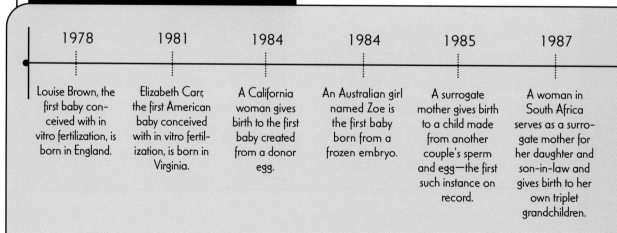

1978	1981	1984	1984	1985	1987
Louise Brown, the first baby conceived with in vitro fertilization, is born in England.	Elizabeth Carr, the first American baby conceived with in vitro fertilization, is born in Virginia.	A California woman gives birth to the first baby created from a donor egg.	An Australian girl named Zoe is the first baby born from a frozen embryo.	A surrogate mother gives birth to a child made from another couple's sperm and egg—the first such instance on record.	A woman in South Africa serves as a surrogate mother for her daughter and son-in-law and gives birth to her own triplet grandchildren.

INTRODUCTION

—their two beautiful children—was worth the effort and the wait: "If it weren't for medical science, we wouldn't have been able to experience the joy of being parents."

Mark and Simone's story is not unique. Each year in the United States, more than two million couples go to doctors for help in treating infertility, which is defined as the absence of conception after six months to a year of regular, unprotected sexual intercourse.

The number of infertile couples has increased in recent years. For decades, it was typical for married couples to have children in their twenties. Today many couples are waiting until they are in their thirties or even their forties to have children. Unfortunately, as women age, they are less likely to become pregnant. When a woman is twenty-five years old, she has a 95 percent chance of conceiving naturally. When she reaches forty-five, that number decreases to 30 percent.

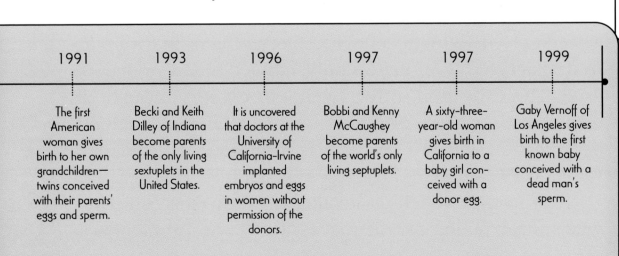

1991	1993	1996	1997	1997	1999
The first American woman gives birth to her own grandchildren—twins conceived with their parents' eggs and sperm.	Becki and Keith Dilley of Indiana become parents of the only living sextuplets in the United States.	It is uncovered that doctors at the University of California-Irvine implanted embryos and eggs in women without permission of the donors.	Bobbi and Kenny McCaughey become parents of the world's only living septuplets.	A sixty-three-year-old woman gives birth in California to a baby girl conceived with a donor egg.	Gaby Vernoff of Los Angeles gives birth to the first known baby conceived with a dead man's sperm.

FERTILITY TECHNOLOGY: THE BABY DEBATE

There are a number of reasons why a couple might not be able to conceive. Regardless of the reasons why (which are discussed in chapter 2), it can be heartbreaking for a couple that wants children to learn that they cannot conceive on their own. Many such couples turn to doctors known as reproductive endocrinologists, who specialize in fertility treatments. With the help of these physicians, infertile couples have many options for helping them to conceive. Together, these medical options are referred to as assisted reproductive technologies (ART).

Infertility is an age-old problem. In the Old Testament of the Bible, Sarah, the wife of the patriarch Abraham, resorted to what today would be considered a form of surrogacy. (A surrogate is simply a substitute.) When she was unable to conceive, Sarah "offered" her servant Hagar to Abraham, and Hagar conceived and bore Abraham a son, Ishmael. (Later, Sarah got jealous and cast Hagar out into the wilderness.)

Over the centuries, women have used a number of folk remedies to help them conceive, everything from catnip tea to drinks made from mare's milk, rabbit's blood, or sheep's urine. The early part of the twentieth century brought an elementary version of today's more high-tech artificial insemination: A man's sperm was inserted into a woman's vagina with something that resembled a turkey baster.

A procedure called donor insemination first came into widespread public use in the 1940s. If the problem was with her partner's sperm, a woman could use another man's sperm for conception. Donor insemination still takes place today, and it is estimated that nearly one million babies have been born as a result of this procedure.

Until 1978, there was relatively little doctors could do to help infertile couples conceive. That was the year that the world's first "test-tube baby" was born. Doctors in England succeeded in performing in vitro fertilization by taking an egg from the mother's ovary, fertilizing it with her husband's sperm in a laboratory petri dish, and placing the fertilized egg in the mother's uterus. Nine months later, a healthy baby girl was born. It was the birth of a period of exciting new developments in reproduction technology, as well.

In the twenty years since the first successful in vitro fertilization, scientists have improved and expanded ART. But with these advances has come a great deal of controversy and debate.

For example, many high-tech infertility treatments cost a significant amount of money, and they are not always covered by insurance plans. Is it fair that only those who can afford such treatments have an opportunity to increase their chances of having children?

Is there a point at which ART becomes too much help? For example, in 1997, Bobbi McCaughey of Carlisle, Iowa, with the help of fertility drugs, gave birth to the world's first living septuplets. The pregnancy endangered the mother's health, and the newborns were at great risk for major health problems.

Or what about surrogate mothers? For example, does a woman who conceives and carries a baby for another couple have any parental rights to the baby once it is born?

As medical science continues to progress, important ethical, legal, and scientific questions about fertility technology will continue to be raised. These questions will rarely have one clear or simple answer.

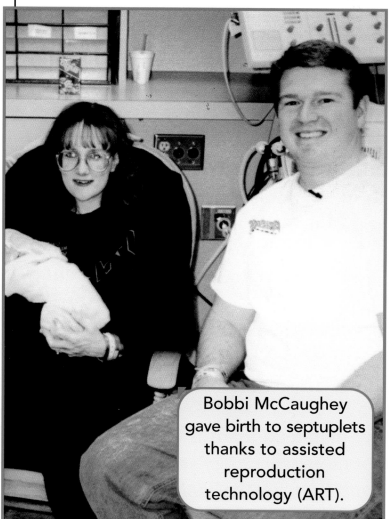

Bobbi McCaughey gave birth to septuplets thanks to assisted reproduction technology (ART).

SEX ED. 101

Before you can begin to understand the science of high-tech infertility treatments, you need a basic understanding of the male and female reproductive systems and how conception occurs.

The Female Reproductive System

Each part of the female reproductive system plays an important role in the conception and development of a fetus.

Vagina and Cervix

The vagina, or vaginal canal, is the opening to a woman's inner reproductive organs. When a woman has sexual intercourse, this is where the man's penis enters. This is also where the baby emerges during childbirth.

At the innermost part of the vagina is the cervix. The cervix is the narrow "neck" of the uterus. When a woman gives birth, the cervix softens and expands enormously so that the baby can come out. A small amount of mucus is normally present in the cervix.

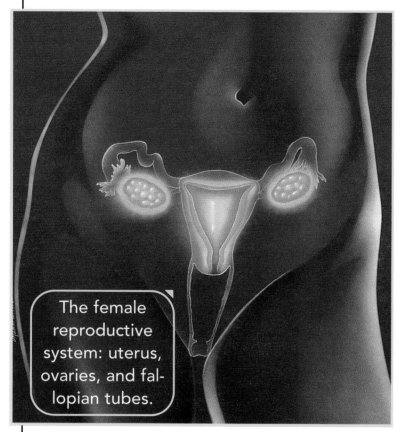

The female reproductive system: uterus, ovaries, and fallopian tubes.

Uterus, Ovaries, and Fallopian Tubes

At the top of the vaginal canal, just below a woman's bladder, are the uterus, ovaries, and fallopian tubes.

The uterus is the muscular organ that holds the growing fetus during pregnancy. When a woman is not pregnant, it is only about as big as a closed fist.

The ovaries are two small organs on either side of the uterus. They contain the eggs, or ova. When an egg is fertilized by a man's sperm, it grows into a fetus. The ovaries are about the size and shape of unshelled almonds. The fallopian tubes are narrow tubes that lead from each ovary to the uterus. These are the tubes through which an egg travels each month from the ovary to the uterus. They are about four inches long.

The Male Reproductive System

The purpose of the organs of a man's reproductive system is to produce and store sperm. Most often through sexual intercourse, that sperm is delivered to the female reproductive system. Conception occurs when the male's sperm fertilizes one of the woman's eggs.

Testicles, Sperm Cells, and Epididymis

The testicles (or testes) are two small organs in which sperm cells are produced. They are located in the scrotum, a loose pouch of skin that hangs outside of the man's body. Because sperm cells thrive at a temperature of 95 degrees, which is slightly lower than normal body temperature, the scrotum's location outside of the body is an advantage.

Sperm cells are many times smaller than a woman's eggs. Each is shaped like a tiny tadpole. The head contains the genetic material, and the long, whiplike tail helps move the sperm along inside the woman's reproductive tract during conception.

The epididymis covers part of each testicle. This is where sperm cells mature and are stored.

Vas Deferens, Seminal Vesicles, Prostate Gland, and Urethra

The vas deferens is the long, narrow tube through which sperm pass on their way out of the body during ejaculation.

The seminal vesicles are small glands located just behind the bladder. They secrete the seminal fluid—the semen—that helps lubricate and nourish sperm cells. This fluid makes up about 60 percent of the volume of ejaculated semen.

The prostate gland is located just below the bladder. As sperm pass through, the prostate secretes more fluid to aid the sperm's passage out of the body during ejaculation.

The urethra transports both urine and semen. A nerve reflex blocks the bladder to prevent urine from passing through the urethra during ejaculation.

Penis

The penis is the organ through which semen exits during ejaculation. During sexual arousal, the blood vessels in the penis relax and dilate, causing it to stiffen and become erect.

Conception

A healthy adult woman carries about 400,000 eggs in her two ovaries. In the middle of a woman's menstrual cycle (which is usually twenty-eight days long), hormones trigger an egg to be released from an ovary and swept into one of her fallopian tubes. This is called ovulation. This is the stage at which conception can occur.

Semen contains hundreds of millions of sperm cells. In sexual intercourse, semen enters the vagina when the man ejaculates. The sperm cells make their way through the cervix and uterus and into the fallopian tubes. While millions start this journey, only a few hundred actually make it to the tubes, which is why the motility—the ability to move—of a man's sperm is as important as his sperm count.

The sperm cell that reaches the egg penetrates the outer membrane and lodges its head inside. This is fertilization. The fertilized egg—first called a zygote and then an embryo—makes its way through the fallopian tube and finally into the uterus, about five or six days after ovulation. When it reaches its final destination, it

BEAUTIFUL EGGS FOR SALE

A Los Angeles fashion photographer named Ron Harris caused quite a stir in 1999 when he created a Web site on which he offered models' eggs to the highest bidders. The site, called "Ron's Angels" is aimed at would-be parents who are willing to spend up to $150,000 for the chance to have an attractive child.

To some, the concept of selling eggs is detestable. Egg donors are usually compensated $2,000 to $4,000 for their time, inconvenience, and discomfort. The American Society for Reproductive Medicine says compensation should not vary based on attributes that the child may or may not have. The group says the Web site promotes unrealistic expectations to potential parents (who is to say a child would inherit the model's genes for beauty, anyway?) and offers undue enticement to potential donors.

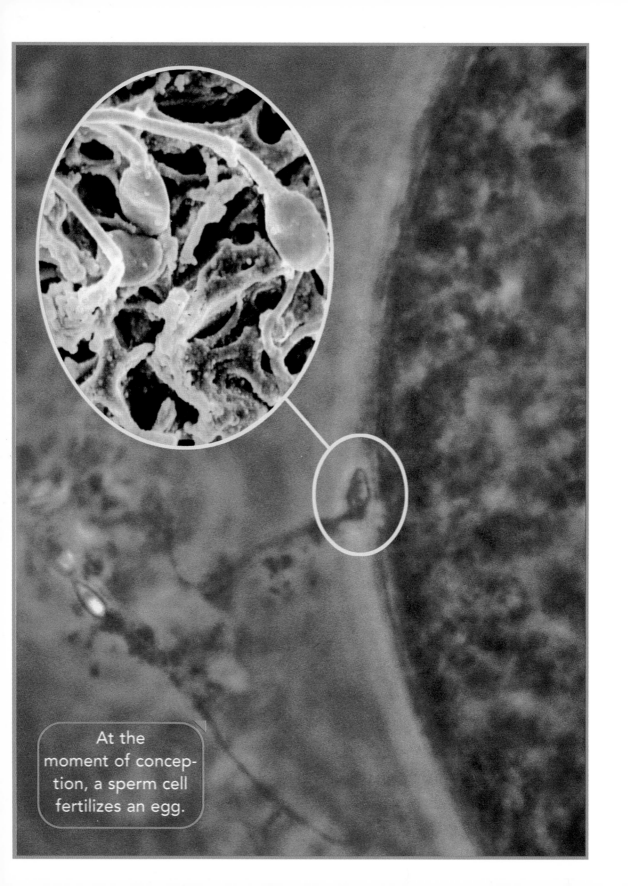

At the moment of conception, a sperm cell fertilizes an egg.

implants itself into the lining of the uterus, the endometrium. There it will stay as the embryo grows into a baby, which will be delivered nine months later.

Perfect Timing

So as you can see, conception depends a lot on timing. If a couple is trying to conceive a child, the best time for them to have sexual intercourse is during the one or two days before ovulation. That way there can be a healthy supply of sperm—which live for up to seventy-two hours in a woman's body—in the fallopian tubes when an egg, which only lives for up to twenty-four hours, is released.

That is not to say that all couples can rely on "timing it just right" as a method of birth control. Many adult women have irregular cycles, meaning for one cycle the wait between periods might be twenty-five days, and for the next cycle it might be thirty-three days. That makes it difficult for them to pinpoint when they ovulate. (Normally ovulation occurs fourteen days before their next period—but if a woman does not know when her next period will occur, she cannot know when she will ovulate.)

Most teenage girls have rather irregular cycles. Most women do not have their periods at regular intervals until they reach their mid- to late-twenties. So at any given time, a teenage girl cannot be sure that she will not get pregnant.

CHAPTER 2

WHEN CONCEPTION DOES NOT HAPPEN NATURALLY

For 7 to 10 percent of all couples in the United States, conception will not result from intercourse, even if they have sex at the time of the month that ovulation is supposed to occur. There are many possible explanations.

Ovulation and Sperm Problems

Forty percent of all infertility cases are caused by problems with a woman's ovulation or a man's sperm. A woman may not ovulate consistently—or at all. Problems with regular ovulation could be caused by inappropriate body weight (too high or too low), drug use, stress, cystic ovaries, or pelvic infections.

As was mentioned earlier, a woman's age does affect fertility. As a woman ages, the number of ova she has decreases—from 400,000 in her early twenties to 200,000 at about the age of forty. Because the quality of a woman's eggs deteriorates as she ages, it may be that the eggs she does release are incapable of being fertilized.

A man may produce an abnormally low amount of sperm cells in his semen; his sperm cells may be abnormally shaped; or his sperm motility may be low—the sperm cells just don't move quickly enough. All of these problems reduce the likelihood of a healthy sperm cell reaching an egg. Causes for

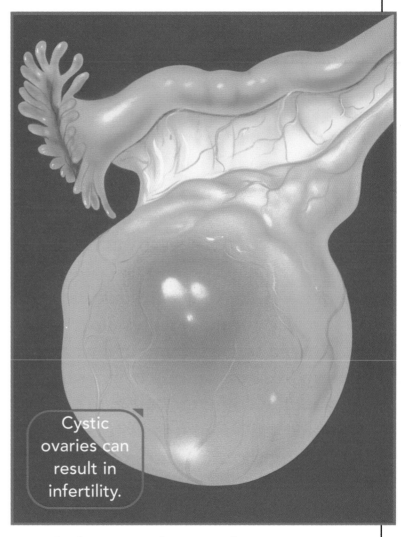

Cystic ovaries can result in infertility.

these problems can include a condition where a varicose vein develops in the veins leading from the testicles; infections; or a blocked vas deferens, the tube that carries sperm from the testicles to the urethra.

Cervix, Uterus, Fallopian Tube Problems

Other difficulties with infertility may result from problems with other parts of a woman's reproductive system. She might have problems with her cervix, for example. If the cervix does not stay closed during pregnancy, the woman will not be able to carry the baby to full term. Or the mucus found around the cervix might be "unfriendly" to incoming sperm. It could be too thin or too thick or too acidic to allow the sperm cells to make their journey.

A woman might also have trouble with her fallopian tubes or uterus. Fallopian tubes can be permanently damaged by an infection (a sexually transmitted disease, for example). If the tubes are damaged or blocked, there is no passageway through which sperm can travel to reach an egg. Fibroid tumors found in a woman's uterus may keep an embryo from implanting or growing correctly.

Another common cause for infertility in women is a condition called endometriosis. This occurs when the lining of the uterus migrates outside the uterus and implants itself in the pelvic cavity. There it can attach itself to the fallopian tubes or ovaries, causing damage.

No Explanation

For about 15 percent of infertile couples, no cause can be found. This is called unexplained infertility.

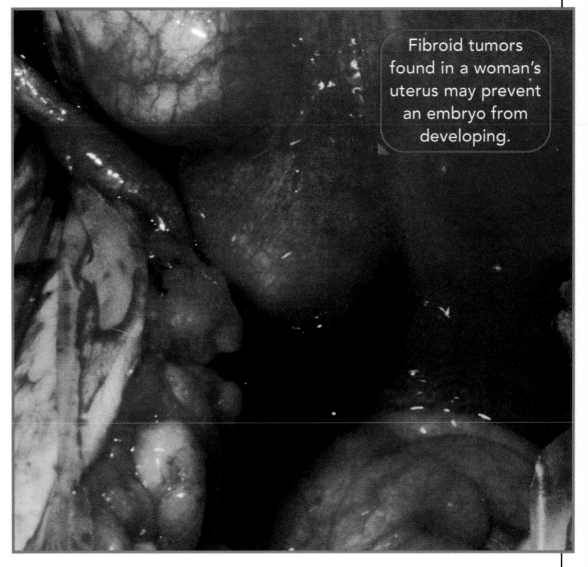

Fibroid tumors found in a woman's uterus may prevent an embryo from developing.

No matter what the reason is for a couple's infertility, it is important to remember that the problem is nobody's "fault." Infertility is a medical condition for which couples must receive medical treatment, just as they would for any other physical problem, in order for them to conceive.

CHAPTER 3

PREGNANCY WITH THE HELP OF SCIENCE

With a doctor's help, a couple can determine why they are not getting pregnant on their own. Once that has been done, the couple can decide whether they want to enlist the help of science in conceiving. Their doctor (most often a reproductive endocrinologist) can present them with the various options that modern medicine offers. There are a number of different options, ranging from nonsurgical and relatively inexpensive to invasive and very expensive.

Low-Tech Methods

Depending on a couple's diagnosis, they may be able to conceive using low-tech medical assistance. These procedures do not require surgery, and they are generally less expensive than the high-tech fertility treatments.

The most common low-tech methods are discussed on the following pages.

Fertility Drugs for Women

Often, fertility drugs are the first step in infertility treatment. Doctors prescribe fertility drugs for millions of women each year. For women who have ovulation problems, these drugs may be all the medical treatment they need to conceive.

The drugs are marketed under such brand names as Clomid, Pergonal, Metrodin, and Parlodel. They promote ovulation by stimulating

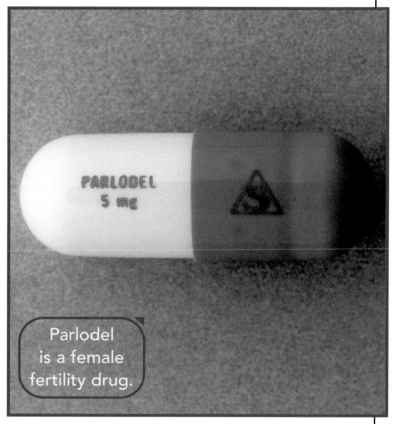

Parlodel is a female fertility drug.

hormones that cause the woman to release an egg from her ovaries every month. They come in pill or injection form. Many of these drugs have been used safely and successfully for more than thirty years.

Depending on the dosage and combinations, fertility drugs can cause more than one egg to be released. If more than one egg gets fertilized at a time, this can cause multiple births (twins, triplets, or even more). Bobbi McCaughey was taking the drug Metrodin when she and her husband conceived their now famous septuplets.

The success rate for women's fertility drugs is high. About 70 to 90 percent of the women who are prescribed the medications for ovulation problems do ovulate, usually within three months of beginning treatment. Of those who ovulate, 20 to 60 percent will conceive. Costs can range from $30 for one cycle of the pill Clomid to $5,000 for a cycle of drugs that are injected.

Fertility Drugs for Men

Men also can take fertility drugs. In many cases, these are the same drugs that are given to women. In men, they act either to signal the body to start sperm production or to promote more or better sperm production.

Although in many cases these drugs are sufficient to enable a couple to conceive, the success rate for fertility drugs in men is not as high as it is for women. When a man uses fertility drugs, the couple's pregnancy rate is about 20 to 25 percent. Costs range from $30 for a cycle of Clomid to $2,000 for a cycle of injections (this is lower than the cost for women because men get fewer injections per cycle).

WHO ARE BABY JAYCEE'S PARENTS?

John and Luanne Buzzanca wanted children, but couldn't conceive on their own. They hired a surrogate mother, Pamela Snell, who carried a baby created with donor sperm and a donor egg. John, Luanne, and Pamela signed a contract stating that John and Luanne would be parents to the baby after it was born.

A month before Jaycee's birth, John filed for divorce. After the birth, Luanne filed for child support, but John refused to pay, stating that he was not the baby's father "in any legal sense." A California Superior Court judge agreed. He did not require John to pay child support, because John was not the genetic father, nor the adoptive father, and he wasn't married to the mother at the time the child was born. He said that Luanne was not the legal mother, either. The judge asserted that Jaycee was, in effect, parentless.

Luanne filed an appeal, and the judge's opinion was overturned. The appellate court awarded custody to Luanne, and required John to pay child support. The court ruled that in signing the surrogacy agreement, John was responsible for Jaycee's conception. John immediately appealed that decision.

The courts' different rulings show that without laws or precedent for such entangled custody cases, there are many different ways to interpret parenthood. With few laws governing surrogacy or other infertility treatments that involve many people, it is likely there will continue to be different opinions in these cases.

Artificial Insemination

With this method, also known as intrauterine insemination, doctors insert sperm directly into a woman's uterus. This procedure might be used when a woman has trouble conceiving due to a problem with her cervical mucus or when a man's sperm has low motility and cannot make the long journey to the egg.

Using an ovulation detection kit (which can be bought over the counter at a pharmacy) or an ultrasound machine, the doctor determines the time of ovulation. Once the woman ovulates, the man produces a sperm sample into a sterile container. The sperm is "washed"—a process whereby the "best" sperm is concentrated into a small pellet. The doctor then inserts a catheter into the woman's vaginal canal, through the cervix, and into the uterus. The pellet of sperm is pushed through the catheter and deposited in the uterus near a fallopian tube.

Conception occurs in about 5 to 25 percent of all intrauterine inseminations. The average cost ranges from $200 to $500 per cycle. To improve the odds of becoming pregnant, a woman may take fertility drugs to stimulate her ovaries to develop several mature eggs instead of just one. In such cases, the cost can reach $5,000 per cycle if injectable fertility drugs are used.

Donor Insemination

Donor insemination works the same way artificial insemination does, except that the woman receives sperm from an acquaintance or an anonymous donor rather than from her partner.

Couples might turn to donor insemination if the man does not produce healthy sperm or if couples are both carriers of genetically inherited diseases. Single women who want to become pregnant but do not have a partner also use donor insemination.

Anonymous donors provide semen to facilities called sperm banks. Today all sperm is tested for the human immunodeficiency virus (HIV). The sperm banks usually provide a medical history of each donor. Sometimes, they also give additional information about the donor's physical traits, hobbies, education, and profession. Each donor usually signs away any legal right to a child born with his sperm. The average cost is $200 to $500 for the insemination procedure, plus about $50 to $75 for the donated sperm. The cost can reach $5,000 per cycle if injectable fertility drugs are used.

High-Tech Methods

If a couple cannot get pregnant with the help of a low-tech conception method, they may turn to one of the following high-tech options to conceive. These methods, also known as assisted reproductive technologies (ART), are more invasive—meaning that they involve entry into the body, as in surgery—and cost much more than the low-tech options.

FERTILITY TECHNOLOGY: THE BABY DEBATE

In Vitro Fertilization (IVF)

This procedure is the most common of all of the high-tech fertility treatments. Couples might use IVF if the woman has a blockage in her fallopian tubes or if the man has a low sperm count.

In 1978, Louise Brown of England was the first child born who had been conceived using IVF. In 1981, the first "test-tube baby" in the United States, Elizabeth Carr of Virginia, was born. Since then, more than 100,000 babies have been born with the help of IVF.

To increase the odds of conceiving, a woman who is about to undergo in vitro fertilization will usually take fertility drugs to produce more than one mature egg. When the eggs are ready, the doctor will retrieve the eggs using a needle inserted through the vaginal wall. Meanwhile, her partner will give a sperm sample in a sterile container.

The eggs are mixed with the sperm in a glass petri dish in a laboratory. Two days later the eggs are fertilized, and each one becomes a ball of dividing cells known as an embryo. The doctor implants two to four embryos (or sometimes more) into the woman's uterus using a catheter inserted through her vaginal canal and cervix.

Usually the doctor implants more than one embryo to increase the odds that at least one will implant correctly and grow normally. Because more than one embryo is usually implanted, there is a 20 to 30 percent chance that multiple births can occur with IVF. Any extra embryos that are created in the petri dish can be frozen, stored, and then thawed for future use if the first IVF procedure is not successful. The first birth of a child from a frozen embryo took place in Australia in 1984.

The conception rate for each in vitro fertilization cycle is about 28 percent. The delivery rate, which means that the woman carries to term and gives birth to the child she has conceived, is about 22 percent. Those numbers vary according to each couple's particular fertility problem and the woman's age. Generally, younger women have higher success rates because their eggs are healthier. In the United States, the average cost of an in vitro fertilization treatment cycle, including injectable fertility drugs, is about $10,000.

GIFT, ZIFT, and ICSI

These procedures are different variations of IVF.

GIFT stands for gamete intrafallopian transfer. It was introduced in the United States in 1984, and about 1,000 babies are born with the help of GIFT each year. The procedure is the same as in vitro fertilization, except that the eggs and the sperm do not fertilize in a petri dish. As soon as they are mixed together, the eggs and sperm are inserted via a fiber-thin tube called a laparoscope into the woman's fallopian tube or tubes through a small incision in her abdomen. There the sperm and each egg fertilize and then make their way to the uterus to implant naturally.

ZIFT is zygote intrafallopian transfer. In this procedure, the eggs and the sperm are fertilized in a petri dish. A day later, the zygotes (they have not divided enough to be called embryos yet) are inserted into the woman's fallopian tube or tubes. The fertilized eggs make their way to the uterus and implant naturally. About 250 babies are born in the United States every year using this procedure.

ICSI stands for intracytoplasmic sperm injection. This is a relatively new infertility treatment introduced in 1992. So far, 2,000 babies have been born with the help of this procedure. Men who have a very low sperm count or who have a blocked vas deferens might use ICSI to help them conceive a biological child.

The procedure is similar to IVF. However, the man does not provide a sperm sample himself. Instead, a doctor retrieves a man's sperm by inserting a needle into his testicle. Then, once a woman's eggs are retrieved, the man's sperm is not just mixed with the eggs. Instead, a lab technician isolates individual sperm and each egg is injected with an single sperm cell. The egg and the single sperm cell are then fertilized in a petri dish and inserted into the woman's uterus like IVF.

Generally, the pregnancy and delivery success rates, as well as the costs for these three procedures, are similar to those of IVF.

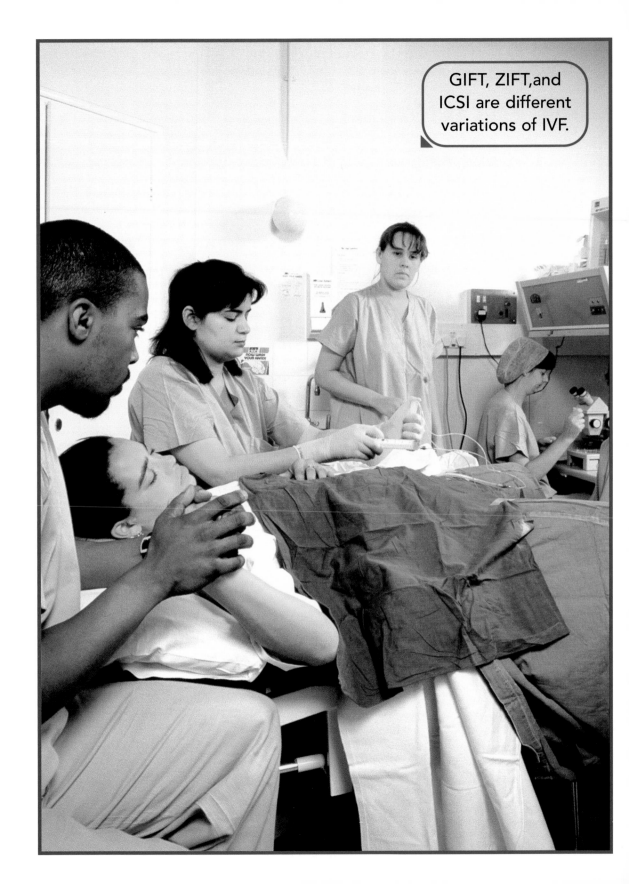

GIFT, ZIFT,and ICSI are different variations of IVF.

Donor Eggs and Embryos

If a woman cannot produce healthy eggs for fertilization, she can use donor eggs, which can come from a friend, family member, or an anonymous donor. If her partner cannot produce healthy sperm, they can use donor embryos made from the combined sperm and egg of donors. Women who have already reached menopause usually turn to donor eggs or embryos to conceive a child.

Egg donors can be found through fertility clinics. Many fertility clinics refuse to offer donor eggs to any woman over fifty-five. However, in 1997 a sixty-three-year-old California woman conceived using donor eggs and her sixty-year-old husband's sperm, eventually giving birth to a healthy baby girl. She had not told the truth about her age to her fertility doctor. The first baby created from a donor egg was born in the United States in 1984.

Usually a fertility clinic will provide detailed medical history about an egg donor, as well as information about the donor's physical traits, hobbies, education, and profession. Once a woman chooses a donor, she and the donor take hormones to get their menstrual cycles in sync. The donor is also given fertility drugs so her ovaries will develop several eggs. When the eggs are mature, a doctor removes them using a needle inserted through the vaginal wall. Then standard in vitro fertilization takes place.

Like sperm donors, egg donors usually give up all rights to any child conceived with their eggs. Couples who use donor eggs or embryos have about a 40 percent chance of getting pregnant. Prices range from $8,000 to $12,000 for IVF, with an additional $2,000 to $4,000 for the donated egg or embryo.

Surrogacy

With this procedure, another woman agrees to carry a baby for the infertile couple. She is called a surrogate mother. The surrogate mother can conceive through artificial insemination with her own eggs and the father's sperm. Or the surrogate mother can undergo IVF and carry an embryo made from the couple's sperm and egg.

A surrogate mother can be found through a fertility clinic, an adoption agency, or a surrogacy agency. Private arrangements can be negotiated with surrogate mothers found in the newspaper want ads or Internet bulletin boards. The surrogate mother could also be an acquaintance or family member.

The first recorded instance of a surrogate mother carrying and delivering the biological child of an infertile couple dates back to 1985. In 1987 a South African woman became the first woman to give birth to her own grandchildren— triplets conceived by her daughter and son-in-law. A similar case occurred for the first time in the United States in 1991: Arlette Schweitzer gave birth to her own twin grandchildren, who had been conceived with their parents' eggs and sperm.

Generally the couple pays for the surrogate mother's expenses, including housing, medical bills, and any agency, legal, or contract fees. The surrogate mother generally agrees to give up all parental rights when the child is born, with the rights going to the father, if he provided the sperm (his partner, the non-biological mother, can then adopt the child), or to both parents, if they provided the eggs and sperm. Surrogacy can be a very complex legal arrangement, especially when the surrogate mother's eggs are used. In some states, surrogacy arrangements are illegal.

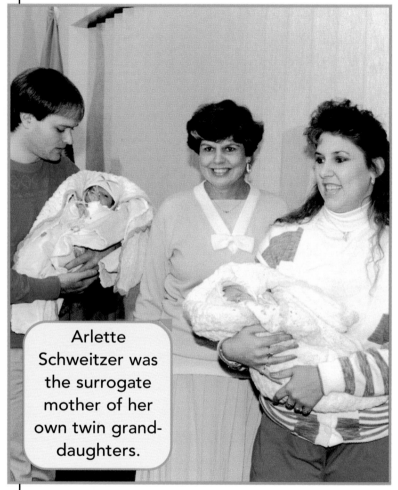

Arlette Schweitzer was the surrogate mother of her own twin grand-daughters.

A now famous court case took place in 1986, when a surrogate mother in New Jersey changed her mind about giving up the baby she had carried for nine months. Mary Beth Whitehead sued to keep custody of the baby, who was biologically hers because the baby was conceived using her eggs. A judge awarded the baby, who became known as Baby M, to the biological father, but Mary Beth retained some visitation rights.

The cost of surrogacy varies, depending on whether the adoption arrangement is negotiated privately or if a contract is arranged through a surrogacy agency. Surrogacy can cost anywhere from $3,000 to $25,000 in legal, administrative, and agency fees, plus $10,000 to $12,000 paid directly to the surrogate mother. These figures do not take into account any fees for an artificial insemination or IVF procedure, or for the surrogate mother's living expenses, prenatal care, or delivery. With these additional costs, infertile couples could end up spending well over $50,000.

IVF SHOCKING STATISTICS

In an effort to cut down on the number of multiple births resulting from infertility treatments, the American Society for Reproductive Medicine recommends that a woman with a good chance of responding to treatment receive no more than two embryos during in vitro fertilization.

Now two years old, three of the McCaughey septuplets rely on feeding tubes for nourishment and/or have severe muscular problems that prevent them from sitting up or walking without help.

According to one study, when you implant one embryo during in vitro fertilization, the success rate is 12 percent; with four, the success rate jumps to 48 percent.

In 1998, Nkem Chuku of Houston gave birth to the first living set of octuplets. One died shortly after birth.

CHAPTER 4

THE BABY DEBATE, PART ONE

In 1978, when Louise Brown became the first baby to be conceived outside her mother's womb via IVF, the world was shocked. This was the stuff that science fiction stories were made of. Scientists called the event a medical breakthrough. Others questioned whether it was right for doctors to "play God." Was it ethical for science to take conception, an event that happens naturally between a man and a woman, and turn it into a laboratory experiment? Some questioned if Louise Brown would grow up to be a "normal" child. Would she be made to feel different by her classmates, or by society at large?

Today, we know that Louise Brown has led a normal life, with no medical complications. And IVF has become a common infertility treatment. Many of the ethical questions, moral quandaries, and legal complications surrounding assisted reproduction remain, however.

People still question to what extent science should involve itself in the "natural act" of reproduction. Many people argue that infertility treatments have advanced so quickly in the past two decades that social attitudes and legislation have not had time to catch up. Many of these unresolved questions concern the issue of high costs, little regulation, and multiple births.

The High Cost of Infertility Treatments

One major unresolved question concerning infertility treatments is, Who should pay for them? The most expensive infertility treatments can cost tens of thousands of dollars. Many people simply

Louise Brown has led a normal life.

cannot afford this kind of expense, especially if their health insurance plans do not cover such treatment.

Currently, there are no national guidelines concerning

infertility treatments and health insurers. Only thirteen states have enacted laws requiring insurance companies to pay for infertility treatments. The type of coverage made available varies greatly: Some insurance companies pay for diagnostic tests but not treatment; others will pay only up to a certain dollar amount; and some cover nothing at all.

What this means is that the most expensive ART is available only to the most economically privileged members of society. Not everyone thinks this is fair. Groups such as the American Society for Reproductive Medicine (ASRM) are working to make fertility technology more accessible by supporting state legislation that requires insurers to provide coverage for infertility treatments.

Little Regulation

Currently there are few laws and regulations governing infertility treatment. For example, there is no governing body that oversees the nation's more than 300 fertility clinics. Although there are laws mandating the maximum age at which a woman should receive donor eggs and give birth, there is no law telling doctors how many embryos can be implanted in a woman during IVF.

The question of regulation is controversial. Many fertility doctors do not want the government passing laws telling them how to run their practices. Would-be parents do not want legal limits placed on their chances to conceive a child. Others believe that the government should stay out of the very individual matter of conception and parenthood. They believe that fertility legislation would violate a couple's freedom of choice regarding reproduction.

Others believe that there must be some degree of regulation governing ART, if only to protect the safety and health of the women undergoing such treatment and the children that are born as a result. The debate over regulation becomes particularly intense when it comes to women giving birth to more than one child at a time.

Multiple Births

In recent years, the number of multiple births in the United States has skyrocketed. From 1980 to 1996, the number of twin births grew by 37 percent. In that same period, the number of triplet, quadruplet, quintuplet, and other multiple deliveries rose 344 percent. Most of this increase is due to advances in reproductive technology.

Because infertility treatment is so expensive, couples often cannot afford several cycles of treatment. They want their first in vitro procedure to be successful. That is why many ask their doctors to implant as many embryos as possible—to increase the odds of at least one developing into a healthy baby. Sometimes, all of the embryos "take," resulting in a multiple birth.

Similarly, when a couple is on fertility drugs that stimulate a woman's ovaries to create more than one egg, a doctor can tell with an ultrasound how many eggs have been created. If a large number of eggs have been formed, the doctor may recommend that the couple abstain from sexual intercourse and wait until the next cycle when fewer eggs develop. Often, however, couples insist on going ahead because they do not want to spend more money or wait until the next cycle to have their child—or, often, children.

It is not only the parents-to-be who want quick success. Fertility doctors want their customers to conceive quickly because it is good for business. A pregnancy becomes a kind of advertisement for the doctor. After all, couples compare clinics' success rates when choosing doctors.

Medical Complications and High Costs

The medical risks for the mother and children increase dramatically in the case of multiple births. While pregnant, the mother is at increased risk from high blood pressure and potentially fatal blood clots. Multiple births often have to be delivered by means of a surgical procedure known as a cesarean section, which can result in complications. Multiple babies are almost always born prematurely, which places them at increased risk for conditions such as cerebral palsy, chronic lung disease, mental retardation, and blindness, as well as for developmental difficulties later on.

That is one of the reasons why there is so much concern about multiple births. The relatively healthy McCaughey septuplets are a rarity. The amount of media attention surrounding the "miracle births" bothered many fertility doctors, who worried that the successful births of seven babies would lead people to believe multiple births are "easy" or "normal."

The cost of multiple births is staggering. One five-year study found that at one hospital the average cost of a single birth is $9,845; twins cost $37,947 and triplets cost $109,765. This explains why health insurance companies are especially concerned about the rise in the number of multiple births. Needless to say, the costs of raising multiple children at one time can be a financial burden for many families.

Selective Reduction

A further controversy involving multiple births is a practice called selective reduction. Doctors abort one or more of the fetuses so that the others stand a better chance of being born healthy. The procedure involves injecting a solution containing potassium chloride into the fetus, which causes its heart to stop beating.

This can be an agonizing decision. Do you put the mother and babies at risk of severe medical complications —even death—in order to try to save all of the children? Or do you reduce the number of babies the mother is carrying to preserve the others? Scientists are researching

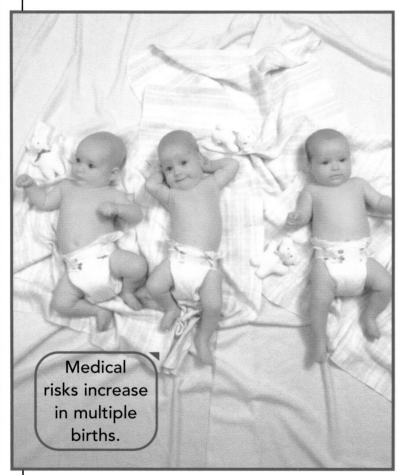

Medical risks increase in multiple births.

ways to make embryos more viable (capable of living) before they are implanted in a woman's uterus. If the odds for embryo survival increase, physicians can implant fewer of them. Current research is focusing on finding a growth environment that will allow embryos to grow to 50 to 100 cells rather than the two- or three-day-old ball of six to ten cells that is commonly implanted now.

CHAPTER 5

THE BABY DEBATE, PART TWO

Cost, regulation, and multiple births are just a few of the issues related to fertility technology with which science and society are grappling. Others include the age at which mothers give birth, custody of children, and deceased men becoming fathers.

How Old Is Too Old?

A major debate concerns when, if ever, a woman is too old to give birth. Under normal circumstances, a woman's ability to give birth ends with what is known as menopause (end of menstruation). For most women, this occurs in their mid- to late forties. But with the use of donor eggs, women in their fifties and sixties can give birth.

Some people argue that just because science has made it possible for women to give birth after menopause does not mean that women should be allowed to do so. Some argue that it is unnatural or against divine will—that if God had meant women to give birth at such ages, he would have given them the capacity to do so. Another argument holds that women should be prevented from giving birth at such advanced ages for their own good and that of their children. The bodies of post-menopausal women are just not equipped to handle the strenuous demands of pregnancy, such reasoning maintains, and older women are less likely to be able to meet the emotional and physical demands of raising a child. Having older parents means an increased likelihood of the child having to deal with things such as the parents' illness, disability, or even death.

The counterargument holds that there is no reason why women in their fifties and sixties cannot be as essentially strong and healthy as younger women, and that what older women may lose in energy and vitality they are likely to gain in wisdom and experience. Older women tend to be more secure emotionally and financially, which can have obvious benefits for their kids. In addition, the argument goes, a woman who makes the decision to have a child so late in life is more likely to be committed to successfully raising that child. And finally, if men can become fathers well into their seventies, why can't women?

In the Courts

The legal system most often gets involved with issues concerning fertility technology when it comes to matters of custody, which means determining who should have the rights and responsibility of raising a child.

The custody of Baby M was one of the first and perhaps the most famous of these court cases. Very few states have laws to deal with cases in which a surrogate mother changes her mind and decides that she wants to keep the baby she carried. In some states, surrogacy arrangements are not even legal.

A different type of custody case took place in 1999. It involved a woman in New Jersey who gave birth to twins —one African American, the other Caucasian. Apparently, her doctor accidentally implanted an embryo that did not belong to her and her husband.

When the woman wanted to keep custody of both children, the biological parents of the African-American boy filed suit to gain custody of him. Ultimately, the court decided to award permanent custody to the biological parents and visitation rights to the other couple.

Frozen Embryos

Often, when a couple undergoes IVF, embryos are created that are not used. These embryos are frozen and stored for future use. It is estimated that there are up to 100,000 frozen embryos in fertility clinics around the country. Many of them were created with anonymous donor eggs and donor sperm, making them, in effect, parentless. There are no laws dealing with "orphan embryos."

Some say that the egg and the sperm constitute a human life and should not be destroyed. Others question the ability of fertility clinics to store so many embryos indefinitely. Does it increase the likelihood that those embryos could become mixed up, lost, or sold illegally?

In cases where the embryos are created by known donors, the parents usually sign contracts detailing what is to be done with embryos that are not implanted. They might be donated to research, donated to other couples, or destroyed.

But what happens if a couple divorces—and one partner wants to use the embryos while the other wants them disposed of? This was the situation in a 1989 court case in Tennessee. The mother wanted the chance to use the embryos to have a child, but the father did not. The court eventually ruled that the husband's right not to be a father overrode the woman's right to have a child. The embryos were destroyed.

Deceased Men Become Fathers

In 1999, Gaby Vernoff of Los Angeles became the first woman to give birth to a baby conceived with her dead husband's sperm. After he had passed away four years earlier, Gaby had had sperm taken from his epididymis and frozen for later use.

Some men bank their sperm if they are ill or dying or undergoing certain kinds of medical treatment (chemotherapy can make a man sterile, for example). Taking sperm from

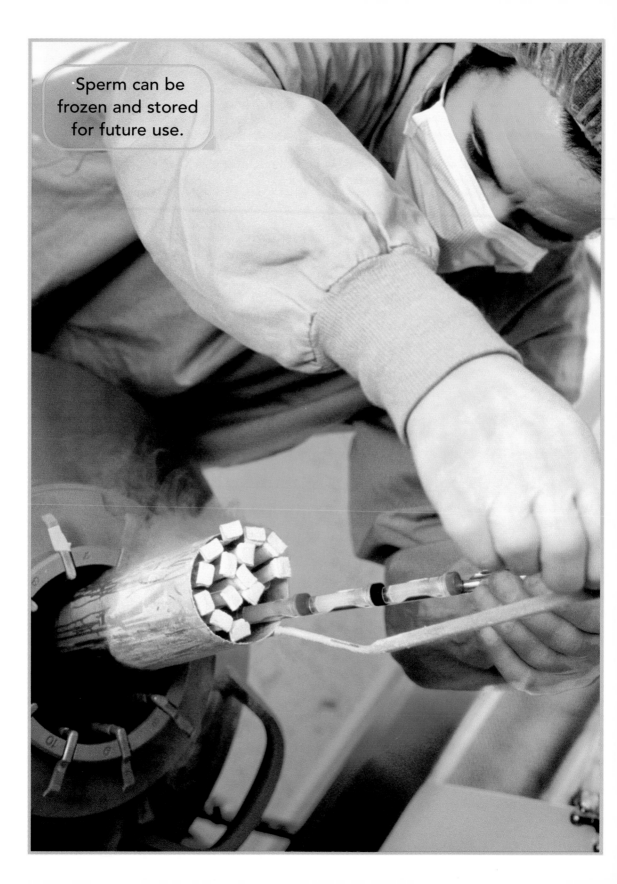

a dead or comatose man is rare, but doctors can perform this procedure if grieving wives or families request it.

Some doctors refuse such requests in the belief that it is wrong or improper to impose fatherhood on a man without his consent. Unless he has agreed to the procedure in advance, a dead or comatose man has no way of letting his feelings be known. The matter can be even more complicated if sperm is taken from a man in a coma. What if he wakes up to find that he is a father?

What happens if the wife of the dead man does not want the sperm, but his parents would like to create a grandchild with their son's sperm and a surrogate mother? Do they have the right to take the sperm? Or, if a woman can take her comatose husband's sperm, what would stop a man from asking a doctor to retrieve his comatose wife's eggs? Finally, what is the psychological impact on a child who was conceived by a dead father? Clearly, there are many questions concerning the use of sperm after death— none of which can be answered easily, especially without legislation governing the procedure.

CHAPTER 6

THE FUTURE OF FERTILITY TECHNOLOGY

Aman gives birth to his daughter… a woman in her sixties conceives a child without the use of donor eggs… parents routinely select the gender, height, IQ, and hair color of their children. Such scenarios might sound far-fetched today, but with advances in fertility technology, some of these scenarios could become reality in the future.

Embryos Outside the Womb

Currently embryos can live in a petri dish for only five or six days before they stop developing. However, scientists are at work trying to figure out how babies might eventually be able to develop outside a woman's womb—carried in some sort of nonhuman container, or in a woman's or man's abdominal cavity, and delivered by cesarean section. If scientists can find a way to nourish the fetus the way a woman's uterus does, a woman's womb may not be needed for pregnancy to occur.

Like today's current fertility treatments, the concept of "growing" babies without a woman to carry them raises many ethical issues. For example, fetuses born in a lab via donor eggs and sperm could be created for the sole purpose of producing organs for medical treatments. Would this be ethical? Should it be legal?

If men were able to safely carry babies without jeopardizing the health of the man or the child, society would need to ask itself whether it is ready for such role reversal. Would there be any negative consequences for the child if his father rather than his mother gave birth to him?

In the movie *Junior*, a man gives birth.

Freezing Eggs

Today, sperm is regularly frozen and thawed for later use. Embryos have been frozen for as long as seven and a half years and then thawed and implanted into a woman's uterus to produce healthy babies. However, freezing a woman's eggs has not been nearly as successful. Unfertilized eggs are more fragile than sperm, and in the thawing process, they become damaged. In 1997 an Atlanta fertility clinic did report the birth of twins who were conceived from frozen eggs, but that feat has yet to be duplicated with any regularity anywhere else in the world.

Scientists continue to work on perfecting the egg freezing and thawing process. For example, success with this procedure might offer a young woman facing the loss of healthy eggs due to radiation therapy for cancer, which can make a woman sterile, hope that she could still become a mother. Frozen eggs would also allow a woman to delay having her own biological child until after menopause.

Designing the "Perfect" Baby

When embryos are created in a petri dish for IVF, they can be tested for certain genetic diseases before they are implanted in a woman's womb. Scientists can do this by removing a single cell from the embryo without affecting its development. Once embryos have been tested, the couple can choose to implant only the embryos that do not carry the genes for genetic diseases (such as cystic fibrosis) or chromosomal defects (such as Down's syndrome). Similarly, scientists can now determine if an embryo carries two X chromosomes (a girl) or an X and Y chromosome (a boy). This allows couples to choose the sex of the embryos that are implanted.

Today, only gender and a dozen of the most serious genetic diseases can be identified in the embryonic stage. However, scientists are currently working on determining the genes (or genetic defects) that cause about 3,000 other genetic disorders, as well as the genes related to traits such as intelligence and physical appearance.

Once scientists determine which genes do what, it is possible that parents could not only reject embryos with certain genes that cause disease but also reject embryos that contain the genes for traits they consider undesirable, such as baldness, nearsightedness, low IQ, and others.

Furthermore, certain genes could be inserted or exchanged for defective or undesired ones. Genes could be inserted for health reasons, or simply to create babies with desirable traits—from blond hair to thinness to athletic ability.

Genetic alteration is a topic that stirs up much debate. Some doctors and ethicists believe that such genetic engineering might be acceptable for medical purposes, such as preventing a child from being born with the gene for a debilitating or terminal illness. However, they find it less ethically acceptable when genetic alteration is used to increase the odds that a child will grow to be tall, for example.

If such genetic enhancement proves costly, as it most likely will, it might mean that only the wealthiest members of society would be able to enjoy the benefits of genetic engineering. The poor would then be left at a "genetic disadvantage." Many people find such ideas disturbingly reminiscent of the plans of the Nazi dictator Adolf Hitler to create a blond, blue-eyed Germanic "master race." Others argue that if parents can give their children an "edge" by helping them along with beauty or brains, why not?

A Final Word

This book has provided just an introduction to the many facets of fertility technology. Over the past twenty years, doctors and scientists have had great success in treating infertility. Even so, these advances are just the beginning. New treatments will be sure to raise ethical and legal controversies just as their current counterparts do, and science and society will continue to question whether the scientific and technological capability to do something means that it should be done.

GLOSSARY

assisted reproductive technologies (ART) Medical procedures used to bring about conception by the use of external means, such as in vitro fertilization (IVF).

catheter A tubular medical device that is inserted into bodily canals, passageways, or cavities.

conception The fertilization of a woman's egg by a man's sperm.

donor insemination Use of sperm from a man other than the woman's sexual partner for the purpose of conception.

ejaculation The release of semen by a man during orgasm.

embryo The fertilized egg after it has begun the process of cell division.

ethical Involving or expressing moral approval or disapproval; conforming to accepted professional standards of conduct.

fetus An unborn baby at the end of the seventh week of pregnancy, after major structures (head, torso, limbs, etc.) have formed.

GLOSSARY

infertility The absence of conception after six months to one year of regular, unprotected sexual intercourse.

intrauterine insemination/artificial insemination Placement of sperm into a woman's uterus to initiate pregnancy by means other than sexual intercourse.

invasive Involving entry into the living body, such as by incision or by insertion of a medical instrument.

in vitro fertilization (IVF) Medical procedure in which the egg is removed from the ovary and fertilized in a laboratory environment, and the resulting embryo is placed in the uterus.

menopause The natural termination of menstruation. It usually occurs between the ages of forty-five and fifty.

motility The ability of sperm cells to propel themselves.

ovulation The release of a mature egg from the ovary.

reproductive endocrinologist A doctor who specializes in diagnosing and treating infertility.

semen A whitish fluid in the male reproductive tract consisting of sperm cells and gland secretions.

sterile Incapable of having children.

surrogacy An arrangement in which a woman (the surrogate) carries a child to term for an infertile person or couple.

FOR MORE INFORMATION

American Society for Reproductive Medicine (ASRM)
1209 Montgomery Highway
Birmingham, AL 35216
(205) 978-5000
Web site: www.asrm.org
E-mail: asrm@asrm.org

International Council on Infertility Information Dissemination (INCIID)
P.O. Box 6836
Arlington, VA 22206
(502) 544-9548
Web site: www.inciid.org
E-mail: inciidinfo@inciid.org

Resolve, Inc.
1310 Broadway
Somerville, MA 02144

(617) 623-0744
Web site: www.resolve.org
E-mail: resolveinc@aol.com

Additional Web Sites

The American Surrogacy Center, Inc.
www.surrogacy.com

Fertility Information Resource List
www.vais.net/~travis/firl/FIRL.html

Reproductive Science Centers
www.reproductivescience.com

Women's Health Interactive Infertility Center
www.womens-health.com/InfertilityCenter/

FOR FURTHER READING

Carson, Sandra Ann, M.D., and Peter R. Casson, M.D., with Deborah J. Shuman. *The American Society for Reproductive Medicine Complete Guide to Fertility*. Lincolnwood, IL: Contemporary Books, 1999.

Cooper, Susan L., and Ellen Sarasohn Glazer. *Choosing Assisted Reproduction: Social, Emotional & Ethical Considerations*. Indianapolis, IN: Perspectives Press, 1999.

Fenwick, Lynda Beck. *Private Choices, Public Consequences: Reproductive Technology and the New Ethics of Conception, Pregnancy and Family*. New York: NAL-Dutton, 1998.

Kearney, Brian, Ph.D. *High-Tech Conception: A Comprehensive Handbook for Consumers*. New York: Bantam Books, 1998.

Marrs, Richard, M.D., Lisa Friedman Bloch, and Kathy Kirtland Silverman. *Dr. Richard Marrs' Fertility Book*. New York: Dell Publishing, 1997.

FOR FURTHER READING

Rosenthal, M. Sara. *The Fertility Sourcebook*. Los Angeles: Lowell House, 1998.

Sher, Geoffrey, M.D., Virginia Marriage Davis, and Jean Stoess. *In Vitro Fertilization: The A.R.T. of Making Babies*. New York: Checkmark Books, 1998.

Silber, Sherman J., M.D. *How to Get Pregnant with the New Technology*. New York: Warner Books, 1998.

INDEX

INDEX

CREDITS

About the Author

Kara Williams is a writer and editor living in Colorado. In her ten-year editorial career, she has covered diverse subjects ranging from colic and child care to skiing and organic farming.

Photo Credits

Cover © Professor P. M. Motta, et al./Science Photo Library/ Custom Medical Stock Photo; p. 2 © Michael Pole/CORBIS; p. 6 © Express Newspapers/7002/Archive Photos; p. 12 © Reuters/Dateline/Archive Photos; p.14, 18, 23, 25, and 44 © Custom Medical Stock Photo; p. 18 inset © Professor P.M. Motta, et al./Science Photo Library/Custom Medical Stock Photo; p. 21 © John Bavosi/Science Photo Library/Custom Medical; p. 33 © Chris Priest/Science Photo Library; p. 36 © Reuters/Jeff Christensen/Archive Photos; p. 39 © Express Newspapers/1255/Archive Photos; p. 49 © John Meyer/ Custom Medical Stock Photo; p. 52. © 1994 Universal City Studios, Inc./Everett Collection, Inc.

Series Design and Layout

Mike Caroleo